Janice

MW01064479

THE PASTOR'S WIFE DOES CRY!

Jesus Can!

Lady B.

7/16/09

By Lady Bea Morgan

Manufactured in the United States of America

Library of Congress
LCNN: 2007929123

ISBN-13: 978-0-9792823-4-8

Cover Design by Majaluk CDM Group
Cover-Photographer Theresa D. Moore-Jackson

Editors
J. Clark
C. McDonald
J. Hernton
M. Bryant

TABLE OF CONTENTS

DEDICATION   *I*

INTRODUCTION   *II*

Chapter 1	*MY PRAYER*	*pg. 1*
Chapter 2	*THE MINISTRY*	*pg. 6*
Chapter 3	*FASTING*	*pg. 11*
Chapter 4	*MY PREGNANCY*	*pg. 14*
Chapter 5	*JEALOUSY AND CONTROL*	*pg. 18*
Chapter 6	*SEPARATION*	*pg. 23*
Chapter 7	*WILLIMINA*	*pg. 26*
Chapter 8	*PAM*	*pg. 35*
Chapter 9	*AIRIKA*	*pg. 45*
Chapter 10	*SPIRIT OF JEZEBEL*	*pg. 52*
Chapter 11	*TWO PERSONALITIES*	*pg. 54*
Chapter 12	*MY MINISTRY*	*pg. 61*
Chapter 13	*LONGSUFFERING*	*pg. 69*
Chapter 14	*ASPIRING FIRST LADIES*	*pg. 75*

TABLE OF CONTENTS

Chapter 15   POTENTIAL FIRST LADIES   pg. 77

Chapter 16   A NOTE TO THE PASTORS   pg. 80

Chapter 17   DEPRESSION   pg. 82

Chapter 18   REJECTION AND ABUSE   pg. 86

CONCLUSION   pg. 92

SCRIPTURES TO COMFORT YOU   pg. 93

DEDICATION

I dedicate this book to all church members who knows not the importance of the oneness of Pastors and Wives.

I dedicate this book to all of you who intentionally exclude your First Lady from prayer as you're praying for your Pastor, not realizing that you are unintentionally praying for her because they are one.

I also dedicate this book to all of you who deliberately exclude your First Lady from information, invitations, presentations, graduations, transportation, communication, congratulations, and consultation. I pray that modification transpires within your spiritual lives.

INTRODUCTION

After the choir sings their last selection, our announcer introduces the man of God, our Pastor. Her joyful, anointed voice that enlightens each listener exclaims, "I present to you our very own! None like him! The "Electrifying Pastor" of the Greater Power Pentecostal Church! Please stand and receive at this time, Elder Claxton William Morgan! The church screams, whistles, claps and hollers as he graces the podium. He stands six feet tall, dark skinned, with "baking soda clean" white teeth, distinguished in his white robe, trimmed in black. When he slowly speaks, the presence of the Lord overtakes the atmosphere. He says, with his beautiful smile, "Thank you, thank you, God bless you wonderful Saints, but now I want you to give the Lord praise." They really begin shouting and screaming then. Even though my husband and I may have had a heated discussion at home, I still stood, smiled, and clapped inspite of, as if all was well. Sometimes I would strain the muscles and nerves in my face and neck to keep from crying. At the same time, foolish, fickle, single women would be rolling their eyes at me in jealousy. But God! I said, "But God," taught me how to leave my troubles at home and how to leave my marital relationship at home. I learned how to separate my husband from my Pastor. That took some adjusting; I managed it, actually, I mastered it!

About nine years later, I learned not only to leave my marital relationship at home, I learned to leave "myself" at home. Just keep reading!

Chapter One

MY PRAYER

*M*r. Claxton William Morgan prayed the Prayer of Faith every week on the Greater Power Pentecostal Radio Broadcast. I tuned in faithfully just to hear him pray. I did not know him. I just turned every radio on in my house so that the power would permeate throughout each room. Prior to ever listening to the broadcast, I asked God for a church home. I wanted to be able to invite people to my very own church. I was amongst a group of young people one day and the Lord gave me a message for one of the guys. The message was that the group he hung with was in danger and that he was to find something else to do with his time, or he was going to be in trouble while with them. About a year later, I asked about the young guy. I learned that he was killed. I also learned that he was in a gang. "If only I had a church to invite him to," I thought.

After listening to the broadcast regularly, I was determined to visit that church on the first Sunday in January, 1994. I remember saying to the Lord, "If I could just get that praying preacher in my house one time, I know that my house would be changed." I was not interested in anything else. Besides, I was just talking. I meant nothing by that. I thought that if this praying man would leave the power of the Lord in my house, then my nieces would stop listening to rap music in my house while I was away. I believed that I would have had more peace in my home.

I did visit the church on the first Sunday as promised and I became a faithful visitor. When I decided to join church, I couldn't figure out when. I was used to hearing, "The doors of the church are opened," but I never heard it and I was waiting for the Deacons to place the chairs out on the side of the offering table for candidates to sit. After carefully listening each Sunday for the proper time to join, I still couldn't tell when by the words that were spoken. They mentioned baptism and the infilling of the Holy Ghost, but they didn't ask us to be a part of the ministry. One Sunday, I made up in my mind that this would be my last Sunday visiting if I did not see the Deacons take a stand and set the chairs out. It did not happen. So as I was leaving the church, I met a lady name Shelley on the stairs. I told her my dilemma and she immediately took my hand and walked me to the Pastor's office to join church. The Pastor made me feel so welcomed. I thanked her. Shelley and I remained friends.

One Sunday, our Pastor, Bishop Louis sent for me by one of his helpers. He wanted to see me and all three of my sons. Bishop said, "The Lord is going to send you some help and he's going to help you raise your boys." I believe that the Lord gave him this message to share with me.

I had already prayed for my husband and in my prayer I asked that he be saved and willing to discuss scriptures with me. I also asked the Lord to show me "my" husband. One year later, I saw the preacher from my church, Elder Morgan, in my sleep. After seeing him, I woke up, turned over, went back to sleep and saw him again. This went on all night, three nights consecutively. I thought that he was in trouble and I thought that I was to intercede in prayer for him. The next Sunday, I anxiously awaited dismissal to speak to him. As I rushed towards him, he too was rushing towards me. He had left the church, but the Lord sent him back to the church to speak to me. He called me during the week and we talked on the phone all night long. I cooked Sunday dinner while on the phone with him, but I did not invite him over. I did invite him over for Thanksgiving. I let my girlfriend talk me into inviting him over after church; I did and he came. Before he left my house, he asked me to date him. We talked about everything. We did everything together. We had so much fun. We fasted and prayed together and it seemed as if we'd known each other for years. Six weeks later, he asked me to marry him. He promised me that he would show me what marriage is all about. He promised me that nothing would ever be more important to him than me. He said that I would not regret marrying him. He said that he would take care of me from every angle in any capacity. He said that no one would disrespect his wife and if a person or persons did not speak to his wife, he would inform them of their disrespect and let them know that we are one.

Claxton assured me that our marriage would exemplify Jesus Christ and that we were going to encourage and counsel couples. We planned a big wedding. We were our own coordinators. We fasted every Saturday for wisdom to better our relationship. He wrote the poem that was on the front of our wedding program and I wrote the poem that was inside the scroll at the reception. Everything went well at the wedding and the reception. We hired every body. We hired the singer to sing as we all entered the sanctuary. We hired the florist to decorate the entire church with flowers and plants. We hired a clean up crew for the church. We hired a decorator for the reception. We hired the caterer. We hired a jazz band. Everything was organized because of prayer and fasting. Our colors were peach and white. There were seven bridesmaids and seven groomsmen. My crazy best friend said that they all looked like pumpkins in their dresses. She thought that they were wide. I thought that they were pretty.

My husband thought about me daily. He talked to me all the way to his job. He called me on every break. We talked his entire ride home from work, and we talked while I cooked. We took walks, viewed movies, and shopped together for large purchases and small. He always had surprises for me and always bought suits and perfume for me. My husband said, "I want to know if you have any concerns or problems with me." He said not to hold anything back from him because he wanted to correct it. He said that communication is the most important aspect of a relationship. He embraced me out of love.

He actually taught me how to love, how to be loved, and how to be in love sincerely. He wanted to know how I felt after we completed different tasks. He wanted to know how he could enhance situations involving us. It was never I, ME, or MY; it was always WE, US, and OUR. He said that there would be no division of any kind in our marriage. He said, "If our bank accounts are different, that meant division. If one goes to bed for the night, the other's evening should end too. Couples should go to bed together. If we should ever have a child together, the child will not sleep with us because that causes division in marriages."

As we know, man's promises are yea or nay, but God's promises are yea and amen! God's promises have not changed yet. Please stand on the promises of God!

Claxton's natural children started visiting us every other weekend. That took some adjusting. His son, Claxton Jr., we call JR, and his daughter, Anita were well mannered children. His two kids plus my three kids took some adjusting. His daughter didn't want to call me by "a" name; she just talked without calling me anything. If the phone rang, she answered and said, "Telephone." I said, "For whom?" She said, "You!" Claxton got her together. He told her to call me Sister Morgan. She was fifteen years old and believe me, I got all attitude from her. She did mean things to me, but I've been through so much other stuff, I can hardly remember all of that. Some weekends she liked me, some weekends, she didn't. Oh, well. JR was only six years old. He just fell right in with the other boys. He was no problem at all.

Chapter Two

THE MINISTRY

Six months after we were married, my husband became the Assistant Pastor of Greater Power Pentecostal Church. I was just getting used to my new family and now he's the Assistant Pastor; this will change everything. Claxton said that being the Assistant Pastor really didn't mean a whole lot. I was relieved. I was excited about him preaching more on Sundays though. Claxton can preach.

Once I got adjusted to him being the Assistant Pastor, six months later, we received a phone call early in the morning. I answered and the lady said, "Tell Claxton he's it." And she hung up. Claxton and I knew that she meant that our Pastor had passed away and that Claxton was now the Pastor, but what a way to spring it on us.

On our first wedding anniversary, Claxton was installed as the Pastor of Greater Power Pentecostal Church. We were too tired to enjoy our cake we had saved from the wedding a year prior. Our honeymoon was over, our dating was over, and our time well spent was over. Claxton was Pastor and I was the First Lady.

We had no idea as to what to expect next. Claxton knew how to preach and he knew how to pray and that's what he focused on. He didn't realize that he was responsible for every area of the church. Other than preaching, he had to deal with the ministers, the ushers, the deacons, the sick, the shut-in, the weddings, the funerals, the finances, the bills, the taxes, the maintenance, the music, the snow days, programs, bulletins, and insurance just to name a few things. We weren't aware. The people knew that.

It was not until Claxton became Pastor that trouble on every hand poured in like a flood. Sadly to say, my husband was too busy to see. Satan had blinded him with busyness. The blind can only see by revelation or healing.

Everyone needed rent money, car notes paid, gas money, utility money, grocery money, Christmas gifts, birthday gifts, graduation gifts, baby shower gifts, and everybody was selling something. Pastor Claxton Morgan thought that he was Bank of America, constantly writing checks. He thought that he was responsible for picking up everybody and taking them home too. Pastor Morgan was used by many. He was busy trying to keep members, they left any way, and some left owing him. Pastor had depleted our savings several times dealing with the Saints. Do you know that none of them came to me to thank me for anything Pastor had done? Do you know that they thought since he was issuing the money, that the money belonged to him only? Do you know how many dinners he paid for? Do you know that the folk he helped didn't even speak to me? Do you know that the people thought that I was living high off the hog? Do you know that some of the women thought that they wanted what I had? Do you know that they never knew how I struggled and I am the one with a husband? Do you know why they didn't know? Let me tell you, it's really simple why they didn't know. It's because they didn't ask, they assumed.

My husband allowed the busyness of church work, employment, and personal friendships interfere with our marriage. When he was upset, I was his outlet. He snapped on me and the kids.

Because of the power that he was given at the church, I believe that he thought it could be used at home too. Communication is to be used at home, but delegation is to be used at church.

Claxton's tongue began to transform into a two-edged sword. I had to pray more for God to bridle mine. I noticed that the devil was using him to divide us and I knew that it was only because he had made multiple promises. I have learned that Satan only tests the strength of something and not the weakness. In other words, if a marriage is strong, that's what Satan will test. If you're the best worker on your job, Satan will test you in that area. If you trust the Lord for a breakthrough, Satan will test you; he'll test your faith. Well, I guess my marriage was strong, too strong for Satan because he is acting a plum fool this day that the Lord has made!

Everybody had to meet with the Pastor after church on Sundays, after Bible class, after prayer, after choir rehearsal, or out to eat. Remember, the Pastor handles the bill. Claxton was attending so many dinner meetings. I asked him about it one day and he said, "I am at dinner meetings with church folk, but we are not discussing church business." I said to myself, "He doesn't know me for real."

I made promises too, but I made my promises to God. I promised God that I would not try to run my new husband over with the car as I tried to do with my first husband. I promised God that I wouldn't get smart with my new husband as I did with my first husband. I promised God that I would not cuss my new husband out as I did my first husband. I promised God that I would be submissive with my new husband and not take control of matters as I did with my first husband. I promised God that I would not disrespect my new husband in the presence of his mother and siblings as I did with my first husband. I promised God that I would not be mean to my new husband as I was with my first husband. I was determined then and I am determined now to go to Heaven. I was not filled with the Holy Ghost when I was with my first husband, so when I was upset, I had flash backs of my childhood and I had raging anger that was uncontrollable. I have rule over my own spirit now. When I'm upset, I know how to quote a verse to comfort me. I know how to call on the name of Jesus. I have kept my promises and it has been a challenge, trust me.

I was angry at God because all I wanted was a saved man to discuss scriptures with. I didn't want to be a First Lady. I cried because I was told that I would have to wear hats, give remarks, introduce my husband, pray aloud, run the Women's Department, sit on the front row, and conduct services. I was too shy for that. I was too nervous for all of that. I had no interest in any of that. I just wanted my family to be a regular family; come to church, pay tithes, sing and clap, fellowship, and go home.

I told my husband how "First Ladyship" originated. I said that there was a Pastor's wife who noticed her husband receiving accolades too often. She observed the many greeting cards and gifts received. She noticed how the Saints reacted to her husband's presence. She noticed how the women basically washed the Pastor's hair with their precious ointment from their alabaster boxes. She noticed that the women had no problem washing the feet of the Pastor's. She said, "Now wait just a cotton-picking minute! We are one! If it had not been for me doing this, this, and thus for the Pastor, there wouldn't be a this, this, or a thus." She said, "I don't care how many women are in my husband's face, in his office, or on the phone, I am the first lady that he sees in the morning, I am the first lady that he compliments in the morning. I am the first lady that he prays with in the morning. Therefore, at church, I'll be the first lady to do for my husband, not any one else. I'll be the first lady to cook for him. I'll be the first lady to compliment him. I'll be the first lady to stand by his side. This means, I need just as much attention as my husband gets. I deserve appreciation services, flowers, birthday gifts and cards, and acknowledgement from everyone. I am first. From this day forward, I shall be called the First Lady of this church!" My husband just laughed at me, but I was so serious. I was angry. All women don't need attention like that and I am one of them.

Chapter Three

FASTING

I desired a closer walk with Jesus. Though I prayed a lot, I wanted more. My friend Shelley shared with me the many fasts that are outlined in the Bible. She also shared with me the many fasts that she partakes in. Shelley is the lady who took me to the Bishop's office to join church. She had an interest in my dreams, visions, and spiritual gifts. In 1997, Shelley introduced me to the Daniel fast in Chapter Ten of the book of Daniel. This fast is twenty-one days of no meat and no pleasant bread. This fast will move Satan out of the way so that we can receive the blessings that God has for us. I have been fasting consistently since then. This was the beginning of my multi-various trials and tribulations. When we fast, the devil knows that the Lord is going to reveal his foolishness wherever the foolishness resides. This is why Satan distracts us when we're consecrated. Satan wants us to become frustrated, doubt God's promises, focus on our troubles at hand and then say, "This fasting is not working." It is important for us to talk back to Satan saying, "Devil, I don't care what problems you may cause today, I am standing on the promises of God." When we're fasting, the Lord reveals unto us the true spirits of those who are close to us. We will better understand their motives, their characteristics, and their darkness. I always want to be in the position to learn about Jesus Christ; His wisdom, His understanding, His revelation, His voice, His behavior, His works, His statutes, His blessings, His love, His compassion, His faithfulness, His miracles, and His anointing. I have learned that if I study Jesus; His attributes, His ways, and His Word, then anything that come up against me, Jesus would make it known unto my spirit. I have learned that if I study He who is Light and He who is righteous, then I would be alright. I also learned that if I study man; his ways, his works, and his word, I'd be in a world of trouble. This is because man changes. Though we sometimes think that we know our spouse and how they will handle matters or we think that we know what they'll say or how they will react to certain situations, we then look mighty disturbed if their behavior is not as we thought. We must remember that the loss of a loved one changes a man; the loss of a job, the loss of a home, the loss of a family, educational incline, financial solvency and insolvency, popularity, marriage, divorce, titles, and positions. So why study man? Man changes. Jesus changes not. He is the same yesterday, today, and forevermore. Study Jesus!

With me already possessing six of the nine Spiritual gifts in I Corinthians 12:8-10, which include the word of knowledge, the word of wisdom, faith, divers kinds of tongues, prophecy, discerning of spirits, my gifts intensified after being filled with the Holy Ghost, fasting, praying, and meditating. Sometimes I frighten myself with my gifts. There are times when I share with friends words from the Lord, dreams, and visions; and they stand in awe. Sometimes, people become jealous of your spiritual gifts, even your spouse. When a person attends a church that does not operate or even understand spiritual gifts, it hinders the work that God has for this individual.

Fasting and meditation causes me to easily recognize unrighteousness; it's immediate! I receive more revelation as I read God's Word while fasting. Scriptures that I have read years ago and have already known had more meaning to them. The Lord gives me parables to write from known and unknown scriptures. The Lord gives me lyrics to songs that I later read in the Bible. I encourage you to fast consistently. Create your own fasting schedule. Form a fasting committee. Write down your purpose for fasting. Write down your expectations of the fast. Write down the distractions you've encountered during the fast. Write down the results of your fasting. Watch God Move!

MY PREGNANCY

When I learned that I was pregnant, I planned a big surprise for my husband. I bought a cake. I made arrangements at a hotel and the hotel employees were going to be in on the surprise. I went to Target to make a greeting card for my husband. I had written a poem as if the words were coming directly from the baby.

He really wanted a baby. I couldn't understand that. I had three boys and struggled with them and then my new husband wanted another child. That was a hard bowling ball to swallow, not a pill. I had gone through being a minister's wife, six months later, an Assistant Pastor's wife, six months after that, a Pastor's wife, and now, two years later, a pregnant Pastor's wife. I couldn't believe it.

Well, I went to the doctor's office so that I could get the results of my pregnancy test on paper for my husband. I am allergic to latex. Why, of all days did the doctor use latex gloves on me?

When I got home, I started preparing for the surprise. All of a sudden, my body began to itch immensely, but it was internally. The itch became aches and it felt like I was having a miscarriage. I called Claxton and told him that I was getting ready to call an ambulance. He said, "Don't call an ambulance, lay your hand on your stomach." He began to pray and ended the prayer with, "Release it, in the name of Jesus." Heat as hot as fire went through my body. Blood clots burst inside of me. I then went back to the doctor's office and they found nothing wrong. Claxton came home and saw me lying on the couch crying.

He said, "What's wrong?" I said, "I was trying to surprise you and the whole surprise was ruined. Claxton sat on the side of the couch and said, "Don't worry, don't cry, we can make another baby, as he was rubbing my back. In the middle of my tears I said, "I'm not crying because we lost the baby, I'm crying because my plans to surprise you were messed up." I said, "I'm still pregnant." He was in shock. I didn't have a chance to tell him that I had gone back to the doctor's office so that's why he still thought we had loss the baby. I said to him, "Let's keep this a secret. Let's let time tell it. You don't have to announce a pregnancy, time does that." He said, "Ok, I'll tell it when the time is right. I gave him the card that I made and he started crying. I am too private for public announcements. I was so glad about our agreement we made on Friday; this was our special secret!

On Sunday morning after the call to discipleship, Pastor Morgan said, "Saints, I have an announcement to make. Where is my wife, somebody escort my wife up here. Ushers, will you please escort my wife up here!" I was always nervous walking in front of people, I was so shy. I perspired unduly and perspiration makes things worst; brown make-up is rolling down my face, legs trembling, and hands sweaty. I did not know why he was calling me up because I knew that he wasn't going to mention our secret that we just made on Friday. I had no doubt about that.

As I was standing in the pulpit, why did Pastor Claxton William Morgan begin reading the greeting card that I made for him? I was too outdone. I was thinking, "Does he know what a secret is?" He said, "Saints, we're having a baby! Then he just busted out laughing. "You all thought that all I did was preached. I do more than preaching and I do more than pastoring." He was cracking up. The church members were happy and many were crying. But then there were some who had a "straight" attitude with me. One lady said, "You told me that you couldn't have any more children." I said, "I may have said that I'm not having any more children, but for me tell you that I couldn't have any more would have been a lie. Besides, I had no reason to discuss with you whether or not I could have more children." The woman got loud with me concerning my pregnancy. Well, we had a little girl, she was named Donnah and she was gorgeous.

Now, my last son was entering kindergarten when Donnah was born. I emotionally and mentally suffered with a newborn at thirty-six years old. I looked forward to my stepdaughter coming over, she was a great help with Donnah. My personal friends and my children all helped me with my baby. Pastor Morgan was busier than ever once the baby was here; wasn't that nice? Did you ask me if Donnah slept in the bed between us? Now you know the answer. Did you ask me how many pampers Claxton changed? Did you ask me how many times have Donnah ridden in his car with him? Did you ask me how many arguments did we have concerning Donnah? Well, what did you ask me? What did I tell you about the promises of man? Didn't I tell you that they are yea or nay?

Chapter Five

JEALOUSY AND CONTROL

When I told my husband about my dreams and visions, He was bothered, as they came to pass. After a while, he said that he didn't want to hear any more of my dreams or visions; that was hard for me. I've been a dreamer since childhood.

I was teaching myself 100 vocabulary words per day. My husband was upset about it. He told me to stop it because all I was trying to do is be smarter than him and he is the one with degrees, not me. Find something else to do with your time. Claxton suggested that I speak in tongues during the day. He said that if I did that, my prayer life would change. Well, I did that and I began to get greater revelation of God's Word; I didn't share that with him.

I learned that when we pray in tongues, we're praying God's mysteries. For he that speaketh in an unknown tongue speaketh not unto men, but unto God: for no man understandeth him; howbeit in the spirit he speaketh mysteries, I Corinthians 14:2. Though we don't understand what we're saying in tongues, I learned that all I had to do was ask God for interpretation. Wherefore let him that speaketh in an unknown tongue pray that he may interpret, I Corinthians 14:13.

The Lord gave me more and more writings. I've written many sermons, books for new members, and I have published my first book on humility. My husband had a fit about my book. He was so angry. Some of the things he said I cannot repeat. I believe that it was all jealousy. Jealousy is a spirit. Jealousy is an unclean spirit. The Bible says that love is strong as death; jealousy is cruel as the grave, Song of Solomon 8:6b. If you know anyone who possesses this spirit, I encourage you to encourage them to fast. Some spirits that have been lying dormant within us for a long time must be fasted out. This may be the spirit that will only come out by fasting and praying.

Claxton's job as an educator enables him to dictate to the children all day long; basically running his classroom as he chooses. No one was going to speak up or speak out to him, he was the teacher. His job as Pastor enables him to be in full control of his church without anyone voicing their opinion or questioning him. Claxton's job at home was for him to be the head of his family; in full control. The difference between the school, church, and home is, if something isn't looking right, sounding right, or feeling right, I inquire about it. The students aren't going to say anything and neither will the church members; they don't have the courage. Though I have the courage, I utilize wisdom as to the timing to address matters with him. It really didn't matter when I voiced my thoughts, Claxton did not want to hear what I had to say. He was used to running everything with no questions. It bothered him when I said, "Did you consult Jesus before you did that?" He'd loud talk me in the car, in the presence of the children or at the stores while we were shopping, it didn't matter.

I'm not argumentative at all, but he surely is. He likes everything done his way or his raging temper is activated. Though Claxton didn't want to listen to me, he pondered a lot of my suggestions, implemented them later, and acted as if he initiated them.

Claxton talked when he felt like talking. We talked about what he felt like talking about and he was angered if I voiced my opinion about it. My children noticed the change in his behavior.

He said mean things to them too. He made a substantial difference between my boys and his natural son. My sons had chores, but his son didn't. My sons couldn't play the video game during the school week, but his son could. He took his son places with him, but not my sons. He expected my sons to be fair towards his son though, and they were. I minister to my own children after Claxton behaves unruly. It's all about control when a person does as he chooses to others without any consideration to the affect that's left on the victims, even when it's your stepchildren.

Claxton made my family feel uncomfortable at our house. For years, my siblings and their kids visited me often. They knew that I was cooking something. That's how it always was. When my family came over, he disappeared in the house until they left or he would leave in the car. I couldn't help that his family didn't socialize like ours.

Claxton also has a problem with my spiritual gifts and

writings. Anything I wanted to do or any plans that I made whereas I needed his support in some way, he would threaten me every chance he got up until that day. At my first book signing, he threatened to cancel it when he was upset, which was daily. So I had to be careful about what I said to him or how I said it; that's called control.

He handled all of the bills and he used to be good with them. Something happened along the way that caused him to go over the budget, making unnecessary purchases, not comparing prices or using coupons.

He is extremely controlling. Being the head of the household differs from being controlling. The head of the house is one who follows Jesus Christ; the controller is one who follows Satan. Nothing is sufficient for him. He was not always like that. Our arguments stopped being fair, he said what he wanted to say and when I got ready to speak he'd say, "Shut up." He'd then leave the room with a threat. "One is given better treatment in the courtroom," I told him.

Pride overshadowed him and it was aggravating. He began boasting and bragging in the pulpit and the members were asking me about it. Even when he announced the baptism of the Saints after altar call, he stopped saying, "I thank the Lord for these wonderful souls that have gone down in Jesus' name. God is always doing great things whereby we must give Him great praise. Four souls have been baptized today Saints; I know that we can do better than that for Jesus!" Then the organ would play and we'd have service all over again. Now he may say, "Saints, bring somebody to church with you next week and tell them that we are baptizing down here at the Greater Power! Tell them that we baptize every week. He stopped giving God the praise. Of course I mentioned that to him and he went "clean" off on me saying that he doesn't boast and brag, God knows his heart. Well, the boasting increased.

When Claxton's behavior began to change, I observed it. That's how I clearly recognized his two personalities.

Chapter Six

OUR SEPARATION

*T*he church made me a married, but single parent; a married, but separated wife. Sometimes, I felt like my husband stopped by the house to pay bills, write sermons, write Bible class lessons, take naps, change clothes, and then leave. He was caught in busyness whereas the busyness became unrighteousness.

The sad part was he didn't realize it. I began to ask God about my situation. I was the mother and the father to my children. I didn't worry my husband with the troubles of the home on certain days of the week because I did not want to hinder his preaching or teaching. Some issues had to wait, although they were important, but other issues were never mentioned. He began to come home with attitudes towards me more often. I'm saying to myself, "How could this be when we hardly see each other?" I could not understand it. Then, he began telling me that I am not a First Lady, I'm just a Pastor's wife. I knew that statement had to come from someone else. He eventually told me that his sister told him that. So when people cornered him to tell him something about me, he brought that home and started arguments with me. Can you imagine members of the congregation talking about you to your husband and your husband believing them?

He said that I needed to talk more at church. He said that the people wanted to hear from their First Lady. I don't know why he was so concerned about the people. I told my husband that if the people really wanted to hear from me, tell them to call me at home, I'm friendly. He came home telling me that the people wanted me to do more and to be more out front. I said, "If you know and they know that I'm shy, why do you allow them to pressure you into pressuring me?" They kept pressuring him about me. We kept getting into it about them. I said, "God is working on me. There will come a time when I will have plenty to say. There will come a time when I will be up front and open too." He said, "I'm waiting on that day." Well readers, eleven years later, the time has come!

I told my husband that he'd rather have a wife in the background fasting, praying, meditating, praising, worshipping, and consecrating than to have a wife flouncing around the church, being seen, being heard, running folk out of the church, gossiping, lying, and deceiving, but yet professing to be holy.

I told him one day, "Ok, you want me to be seen. I am going to come to church in the middle of your sermon, walk down the center aisle, dressed to kill, with a bad hat and coat on, speaking and hugging Saints on the way up, then take a seat on the front pew." "Is that what you want?" He said, "No, ole' crazy fool, that's not what I want. You're just as crazy as I thought." By the way, that was the beginning of the name calling.

My husband did not realize or did not know that spirits transfer from one person to another. When he came home acting a fool, my prayer life increased. He needed to know that if he's in a meeting with someone who is selfish, that spirit could rest upon him. He needed to know that prayer had to be exercised before and after each meeting he had. He thought that I didn't know what I was talking about I guess because I don't have a degree.

It is difficult for my husband to hear what I'm saying. I do have letters behind my name and they are JC which stands for Jesus Christ. That's enough letters for me.

Our communication with each other was declining. He couldn't hear my personal troubles. He only heard the cries of the members. The Pastor's wife does cry! When the Pastor's wife needs a Pastor, who does she go to? Everyone will not understand and everyone does not have Godly counsel for her. What must she do? On one hand, she's trying hard to be the wife she needs to be for her husband at home. On the other hand, she's trying to be the assistant she needs to be for her husband at the church. At the same time, she has many haters (carnal minded women) who think that her life is so glamorous. On top of all that, she still has children at home with their own issues whether it is doctor's visits, sports, homework, or parent/teachers conferences, aside from the sibling rivalry, punishment, meals, and shopping.

Tribulation worketh patience, patience worketh experience, and experience worketh hope. I have a lot more patience than I did. I have a lot more experience than I did. It's all good! It's all God!

Chapter Seven

THE BEST FRIEND WILLIMINA

Willimina is the best friend to my husband, Claxton. They became friends after Claxton's divorce. He was a lonely man with no friends. Being a school teacher, he hated the holidays because he had no one to share them with. He also dreaded summer, winter, and spring vacations.

Willimina knew his troubles so she took advantage of him. She caused him to develop trust in her. She had access to his apartment. She brought food over for him to eat since he wasn't eating often. She was real short, dark, with long thick beautiful hair. She was quiet, not humble; just shy.

She dressed really nice and built up extremely well. She was cute in a sense, I guess looking at her with your eyes closed, she was a knock out. Claxton spent money on her and gave her money. He sponsored many dinners too. She was not interested in dating him because he wasn't her type; he was too old, sang, and hummed all the time. He wasn't too old to spend money on her though.

When Claxton finally decided to date, Willimina had a problem with it. He shared with her information about his new relationship. When the relationship began to sour, he shared that with Willimina. She assisted in his breakup with the lady.

Claxton and I began dating a year or so later. When he decided to tell Willimina about us, we were already engaged. She was destroyed by the news. He finally told me about her and how they became friends. He said that I had nothing to worry about; their relationship was nothing.

Willimina left a message on his answering machine saying that she should have been with him when he picked out my wedding ring. She felt that since they were friends, she was left out. I heard the message myself. I told him that she was in love with him otherwise she wouldn't have clowned like she did. She was so busy thinking that she knew him well, and then he slipped me in. She didn't realize how much she loved him until he was hooked.

She called me a few times to ask me about my wedding plans, but because I am who I am, I gave her no details. At the wedding reception, my best friend, Jester, stood up while we were eating as if something was wrong. I said, "What!" Jester said, "Who is that girl standing in front of us?" I said, "That's Claxton's best friend, Willimina." She said, "I overheard her saying that your dress was ugly. I'm getting ready to beat her down." I said, "Girl, that's alright, don't worry about that." Jester was heated.

As time passed, they remained friends and she became a regular in our arguments. She used to go to Claxton's school to help him decorate his bulletin board. She took fruit and lunch to him on his job. She only called the house when she couldn't catch him on his cellular phone, class phone, office phone at home, or office phone at the church. Of course she didn't like me, but told Claxton that I didn't like her; that's called deception. She brought cake and balloons to the church and had someone to open his office door so that he could be surprised when he entered; wasn't that thoughtful?

She always gave him personalized gifts with engraved special sayings. Everything she did was under the table, under handed, in secrecy, behind closed doors, or behind the scene. She disrespected me as a person and as a woman of God. She disrespected my husband as a friend and as her pastor. She disrespected Claxton's ministry and our marriage.

The Bible says, But he that doeth wrong shall receive for the wrong which he hath done: and there is no respect of persons, Colossians 3:25.

Claxton attended her family outings and dinners. He attended her graduations and celebrations. They are both to blame and they are both responsible for their actions and reactions. He allowed his friend to assist in dividing us and he saw no wrong in what he had done. She caused division in our marriage. She came in between our covenant agreement that we made with God. Claxton's hands have blood on them too.

After we had Donnah Mary, Willimina adopted a baby. Claxton went with her to sign the adoption papers.

Do you know that Pastor Claxton William Morgan announced to the church that he took off from work to be with Willimina on her special day; wasn't that nice? When the announcement was made, that is when I learned of the adoption, when the church did. When I got home, I asked him to explain to me what he had signed. He said that if anything should ever happen to Willimina, then he would raise her son. I told him that he didn't spend time with his natural son or his stepsons. I also told him that I was not raising another child. There's a proper and a respectful way to do all things.

In Willimina's mind, she had a family that she so desired, an adopted son and his dad; isn't that precious?

The following Mother's Day, I had the opportunity to go out of town. This was my first time being away from my children on Mother's Day. After Sunday morning service, I received phone calls from some of the members telling me that Willimina and Pastor Morgan had their special day. Claxton was officially her son's God father. I was told that the service was more like a wedding ceremony. I had to wait until I got back to my hotel room to cry. I was so bothered by that. They, together, openly embarrassed me and disrespected me. Always remember that:

The Pastor's Wife Does Cry!

When Willimina went around for offering, she would hand her baby to the Pastor; service was not over yet. She wanted everybody to know that she had a family; wasn't that sweet? When her son got a little older, she held him up in the air while pointing at the Pastor, as he stood at the podium saying, "See Daddy?" Claxton told me that himself one day when he was mad at her. Besides, the ushers had already told me.

One Sunday, Willimina came to the altar for prayer. As she was leaving the altar, the Lord spoke to me and said, "She's a walking cloud of darkness."

One day in meditation, the Lord gave me a parable about Willimina. The Lord said that she was like a dandelion. He said that a dandelion is attractive; it's similar to a flower in appearance, it stands alone, looking harmless; and the stem is even healthy.

As pretty as grass is after its cut, one little dandelion may be standing in the corner close to the fence. If we pluck it up, another dandelion springs up on another side of the yard. If we take our eyes off of the dandelion, it will take over the lawn. The dandelion can't be plucked up. It has to be rooted up. Otherwise, we'll have one patch of "bald-headed grass" and eventually, we'll have nothing but dirt. Dandelions are weeds and weeds must be destroyed. For our dandelions in the grass, we must buy weed killer. For the dandelions in our lives, we must buy truth, and sell it not; also wisdom, and instruction, and understanding, Proverbs 23:23.

It was difficult convincing Claxton that he was Willimina's friend, but she was not truly his. He could not understand when I told him that he meant more to her than a cordial friend as he thought. I told him that a best friend speaks to their best friend's spouse. A best friend doesn't have a problem visiting their friend at their home. "Willimina meets with you everywhere else, but home," I told Claxton.

A best friend will communicate with your spouse about purchased gifts or outings. I said that she never presents you or us with cards or words of encouragement during anniversary programs, holidays, or birthdays. I told him, "She does not attend any anniversary services and she's supposed to be supporting you?" Then I asked, "Why do you receive gifts from her in secrecy?" He never had answers.

My husband was caught up in an emotional affair. That's why he was saying that he couldn't communicate with me. That's why he was saying that I didn't understand him and all that he's going through. That's why he was operating in secrecy. I told him that she was not a good person to be friends with or to be around especially with her condition (depression). I told him that either she was going to pull him down to her level of unrighteousness or he was going to pull her up spiritually. I told him that she was winning because she was surely pulling him down. I believe that Claxton and Willimina really thought that because they were educated, that they had wisdom; isn't that cute?

Willimina changed churches. Everyone deserves a

change in life, especially if it's for the better. After she attended her church service which was earlier than ours, she'd drop her little boy off at our church every Sunday for Pastor Morgan to baby sit while in the pulpit. When the little boy needed to go to the restroom, the Deacon who was on pulpit duty took him. The Deacons were not in agreement with this set-up. I have nothing against the child; he calls my children his brothers. He'll learn later the real deal. Great commotion was caused by the child sitting in the pulpit, so after a while, it stopped.

I know that all of the foolishness was for the devil to upset me, but in actuality, it increased my prayer life. Let me grace you with a verse that comforts me. Upon the wicked he shall rain snares, fire and brimstone, and an horrible tempest: this shall be the portion of their cup, Psalm 11:6.

Willimina and Claxton were seen shopping at the mall miles away and thought they were safe. If the friendship was so pure, then why hide? If hiding was to keep from stumbling someone, that means that the Holy Spirit had already warned you of your wrong doing, you didn't take heed to the warning.

My husband spent so much money on that girl! Willimina became close to the Pastor's secretary and spent time at her house. The secretary worked from her home. After it was told that Claxton purchased all of the furniture in Willimina's new house, except for the dining room set, he then came to me to tell me that he only bought her a dish washer. Precious reader, did you ask me if I needed one? I thought I heard you asking me something, but I wasn't sure.

He told me that he helped her paint her house. Oh reader, did you question me again? Did you ask me whether or not our walls were once white, but now black and not from paint? Willimina's neighbors saw Claxton at her house everyday and knew that he was changing from his suit to his paint clothes and back to his suit again to come home. I wouldn't call that deception, would you? I would just call it two left shoes.

Willimina's friend, Airika, was also a member of the church. Her profession required no formal education, but yet experience; no excellent speech, but yet confrontational; no dress code, but yet provocative; guess the vocation.

After hearing all that Claxton had done for Willimina, she couldn't miss out on that. She betrayed Willimina and started telling Claxton what his best friend was saying about him. Airika was always in need of counseling from Pastor Morgan. She was always in his office. Then, she played the role of armor bearer for the Pastor. She started carrying his briefcase, turning the engine on to his car, and hanging around waiting for him after every service.

When my husband's family friend learned of all that Airika was doing, she took over. She became Claxton's personal armor bearer. She moved Airika right out of the way. Airika said to Claxton that Willimina said that he could never be her Pastor. His feelings were hurt. As much evil as he does, he has the audacity to be sensitive. Please explain that. Airika caused Willimina and Claxton's friendship to end, but theirs grew. Just hold up, I'll be back to tell you about Airika. Let's talk about the family friend, Pam.

Chapter Eight

THE FAMILY FRIEND
PAM

*P*amela has been a part of the Morgan family since they were children. She is about five foot eight, fair complexion, and medium length hair. She wears binocular-thick glasses, talks fast, stutters, deceives and walks fast. Pam is hyper and she's always moving around.

She constantly goes into her purse searching for something or she's writing something (not notes) or she's talking. This is done throughout the entire church service and remember, she sits in the pulpit; how distracting. Then during altar call, she works the altar, expecting someone to be saved or expecting someone to come to her for prayer. She doesn't even hear the sermons; well, she doesn't listen to them.

Pamela was not a friend to Claxton until they became teenagers. He said that Pam disliked him when they were young. Of course Pamela couldn't stand me, but made my husband think that I disliked her. I didn't even know her. I had no reason to dislike her. She knew then that she was going to give me a reason to dislike her. If I disliked any thing, it would only be the unclean spirit that a person carries.

Claxton and Pam attended college together, receiving

their teaching credentials. Pam is the busy body, but doing nothing really. Claxton thought that because Pam made travel arrangements for all of his trips, reserved rental cars and hotels, that she was an entrepreneur. You don't need extensive training or experience to call the airlines for a flight. I appreciated her assistance, but she wasn't doing anything too challenging, but she surely fooled Claxton.

When we arrived at the airport to depart, we stood at the end of the long line. She would go to the front of the line and holler back to us, "Come on y'all, hurry up," as if she had made a deal with the ticket agent. When we got up to the front of the line, looking crazy, folk stared at us. Pam was fast talking the ticket agent, who was looking lost, and we were getting ready to get the beat down by passengers who had been waiting in line long before us.

As we walked through the doors of the airport, Claxton was grinning and said, "See, Pam knows how to get things done; that's what I'm talking about." I was looking at him, ready to hit him and said, "That was wrong!" Then he said, "We didn't have to wait, did we?" I said to myself, "That's pitiful." I couldn't say too much. The trip would have been ruined. It's important to pray without ceasing.

I was a secretary for years making thorough multiple travel arrangements for military men and civilians. At that time, we had to be sure to reserve smoking-aisle seats or non-smoking-aisle seats, smoking-window seats or non-smoking- window seats. I told Claxton that I know how to reserve hotel rooms and flights. He thought that Pam was excellent at it. How can you think that something is so excellent when Jesus is not in it?

Pam volunteered to be Donnah's God mother while I was carrying her. I asked Claxton what he thought about that and he said, "Well, if she wants to be the God mother, then let her be." My oldest sister taught me a good lesson when I was a teenager. She said, "Be careful with people who quickly volunteer to bring the main dish to a party, or volunteer to sing the theme song at a special event, or reserve the front row seats to the program. That's the very one who volunteers to "assure" you that it won't get done."

Years later, I reminded my sister of the lesson she taught me and it blessed her; she didn't remember it. Well, sure enough, my daughter has a God-mother who doesn't even speak to her. So I know that you know that Donnah has never received a doll, a card, or a sucker. Most God-mothers try to do something for their God-children even if it's just hugging them. Not that I was expecting her to take care of my child like Claxton does with his God-son, but she volunteered; she was not asked. It really should have bothered Claxton because Pam is his friend.

A few years later Pam denied being Donnah's God-mother right in the presence of my sisters-in-law and me. I said, "Pam, it's on video." Then she remembered.

Pam ran members away from the church, especially young boys. The boys are the ones we really need to hold on to, in this day, as much as they are faced with. She told one young boy that he was retarded because he stuttered (didn't I say that she stutters?).

Claxton would never believe the things she did or said, not unless he just closed his eyes to it all. That boy who she called retarded ended up leaving church and has never returned.

My own son was mistreated by her as well. He worked in the sound room at church. When he came home from college for Christmas break, he worked three Sundays without pay. He said that Pam told him that since he left for school, he was off of the payroll. When my son told me that, I went into the Finance Department to see what the problem was. The Deacons told me that Pam was to submit paperwork to them stating who worked on that Sunday in order for them to be paid. She did not submit my son's name. They gave me his money on the spot.

I did not address Pam or Claxton about it. Why wouldn't a person want a teenager to have $25 in his pocket? My brother told me years ago to give my boys money when they reached a certain age otherwise, they will steal. Everybody knows that mothers act a fool over their children. I have been tried and tested over and over again. I don't think that the Saints knew my past.

They think that I've always been saved because I'm quiet. I don't take quiet people for granted, meaning that I want to know their thoughts. When quiet people are thinking, are they thinking on the goodness of Jesus or are they thinking on seeds sown by Satan? This is my philosophy. Make friends with quiet people. If they're thinking on Jesus, maybe they will have a word for you. If they're thinking on Satan, maybe you'll have a word for them. Don't take them for weak, slow, off, crazy, or ignorant. Get to know them.

Pam carried Claxton's briefcase; escorted him to the pulpit; laid hands on him in prayer after escorting him to the pulpit; kept his juice supplied in his office; went in and out of his office as she pleased; went through his briefcase looking for stuff; handed him handkerchiefs while he was preaching and switched clean handkerchiefs with the used ones on the podium. One of the members said to me, "Pam has every base covered to block you from doing anything for your husband." This observation was from a male. She had such a controlling spirit, along with jealousy and envy. Pam encouraged me to study the spirit of Jezebel intensely.

Pam drove Claxton to all of his preaching engagements, Pastor's anniversary services, and funerals. When we held funerals, she drove him to the cemetery when he could have ridden in the hearse. All of these acts of foolishness were done without me; sometimes without my knowledge or consent.

Pastor Morgan was held up so long on Sundays with his clique. I would wait for him so that we could eat together. He started saying, "Just put me some food up. I'll eat it later." When he came home he'd say, "I'm not hungry" or he'd say, "I don't have a taste for anything right now." Then I learned that he was going out to eat every Sunday with his armor bearer and a few other ladies. That was deception! That was the beginning of the end of our family meals together.

Every time Claxton and Pam went to a visiting church, a First Lady would call me to see what was going on. One engagement that they attended, Pam burst through the front doors of the church, stood in the center of the aisle, made a call on her cell phone to the lady in her vehicle and said, "The coast is clear. The Pastor may enter." Remember, the service was in session.

When the First Lady called me, I was too embarrassed. She said, "Girl, you would have thought that the U.S. President had arrived." Claxton is too distinguished for foolishness. I told him that when he and Pam enter a church, she makes his expensive suits look cheap.

Claxton's name was being destroyed throughout our District. His reputation was damaged. The Bible says let not then your good be evil spoken of, Romans 14:16. My husband could not see the danger that was ahead of him.

I was angry about so many issues, but didn't have the time to dwell on one issue in particular. I was concerned about his name being ruined. It looked as if Claxton and Pam were dating though I never believed that. I spoke with her once at the church and told her, "If my friend was walking in error, I would tell him." I also told her, "It's not you that I dislike; it's all of the unclean spirits that are upon you." We were supposed to get together later to talk, but Claxton told her not to communicate with me.

One year, Pam planned the Pastor's anniversary service and it was different. There was a power point presentation that was really nice. Prior to the anniversary, pictures were taken of the members and brief oral presentations were made.

Out of all of the pictures, there was not one of my sons, or my stepchildren. There was a picture of our daughter, Donnah and his God son. There was also one picture of me standing sideways, far back, and looking midnight black and fat. The picture of Donnah was cute. Everybody sighed simultaneously because Claxton was putting her barrette on her ponytail. Now you know that Claxton does not comb Donnah's hair. It looked as if they had this perfect father daughter relationship. That was deceiving because Claxton is never home to see her hair much less comb it!

Pam was responsible for setting up microphones and controlling the volume. Why is it that the microphones always worked fine during the opening prayer, praise and worship, and announcements, but when I took the podium to lead a song, the microphones went out? The microphone was turned down, turned off, or had too much bass or treble.

Pam's child was actually sitting in the sound room as she sat in the pulpit. They had hand signals and codes that they used to control the sound. She exercised every signal and code when I got up. My husband never addressed this matter. When he took the podium, he said, "I need more volume on my microphone and take some of that bass out, please." Claxton knew, but he didn't stop her.

One song I led, I went through four microphones. I didn't realize it. All I remember is one of the ministers kept handing me a microphone. If she knew the prayers that I have over my singing voice, I don't believe that she would have performed in that manner. While I'm singing, I expect souls to be saved, shackles to be loosened, chains to be broken, minds to be changed, hearts to be mended, strongholds to be pulled down, natural and spiritual sight to be given, the lame to leap and not just walk, the sick to be recovered, the dumb to sing and not just speak, healing of broken hearts, lifting up of bowed down heads, and unclean spirits to be cast out. I expect for God's presence to be so thick in the sanctuary that everybody will know that Jesus is in the house.

The devil used Pam to hinder the Lord's work. Though the microphones were out, Jesus still took over. I can't see the people while I'm singing, but I can feel the presence of the Lord and I can hear the uproar of the people in worship.

When church is dismissed, someone would always come to me saying how they were blessed by my singing.

I don't have a beautiful voice to me, but that doesn't matter because as long as I'm singing for Jesus, sweet smelling savor fills the room. A beautiful voice with no anointing is nothing but tinkling brass.

One Sunday evening, one of the musicians and I were in the pulpit waiting for the program to begin. As we were talking, the musician asked Pam to get us a program from the Ushers because they sometimes forget to place them in the pulpit. Pam said, "Get who a program? I'll get you one, but I'm not getting anybody else one." She kept her word. She brought the musician a program and said, "Here!" The musician in turn handed it to me. I smiled. That did not bother me at all. The Lord didn't allow me to be hurt or embarrassed. But when I got home, I remembered the incident and got mad. I was glad that I was at home. I have not forgotten how to cuss; I just choose not to cuss.

On the following Wednesday, I entered the church from the basement. As I attempted to walk up the stairs to the sanctuary, Pam was also walking up the stairs, but with the assistance of some of the Saints; she was on crutches. They were taking up the entire stairway and it caused me to wait. The devil said to me, "Say to her to move out of your way." The Lord said, "Just wait, she should have given you a program on Sunday."

One Sunday, as I was ushering, The Lord spoke to me and said, "Where is Pam?" I began to search the church from my post. I did not see her. Usually, when she's at church, she's in the pulpit. The Lord impressed upon me to leave church earlier than usual. I told my kids to watch me for our exit.

As we rushed out of the church, why was Pam sitting in her vehicle directly behind my car? Why was my windshield cracked? When I told my husband about it he said, "Well, it wasn't cracked on Saturday because I drove it." He knew, I knew, and Jesus knew.

Because of Pastor Morgan's reputation, he wasn't getting speaking engagements as he once did. Guess what, he blamed me for that. He thinks that I have made calls to First Ladies to pull his name down. Did he forget that he rode with his armor bearer, Pam, to many churches without me? I did not have to make calls to destroy him when he made personal contacts with these Pastors and First Ladies at their church. Pam was so busy trying to hurt me, she was really hurting Claxton.

Chapter Nine

THE FRIEND OF THE BEST FRIEND AIRIKA

*A*irika thinks that she's me. I am honored that one would go out of their way to dress like me and desire to be like me; I'm flattered.

She's built up really nicely and she knows it. She used her body quite well and not in a holy manner. Some women think that man's only interest is their body; this is the carnal minded woman of course. If only she would take a moment to think. I was going to say, "If only she would utilize wisdom," but, I couldn't because wisdom comes from God and carnal minded women are not getting applied knowledge from God. So anyway, if only a woman knew that if a man's vital concern or interest is her body, he will take the first train out of Indiana when that body breaks down. When she becomes overweight, underweight, wrinkled, grey, baggy, toothless, bald, limbless, tangle eyed, scarred, bruised, or deformed, it's prayer time for her when men are not double-looking at her, especially if all she had going on for herself was her fabulous body.

If a man's main concern is the woman's love and faithfulness to Jesus Christ and all of His commandments, statutes, precepts, laws, judgments, ways, power, spiritual gifts, and fruits of the Spirit, wouldn't their relationship be more trusting, loving, promising, and blessed?

Airika betrayed her friend Willimina, to become friends with my husband. Isn't that a wonderful friend to have?

She started cooking for him. I don't know how much of her cooking he has had, but I do remember her sending Claxton, by one of the ministers, one slice of lasagna and one half slice of Texas toast. I was sitting in the car with one of our members who had ridden with us to hear the Pastor preach. The minister handed me the food and told me who it was from. She just hugged me inside of the church and said, "Praise the Lord, First Lady." She could have handed me the food. I was heated because of the deception.

When Claxton got into the car, I said, "Here." He said, "What's that?" I said, "Food from Airika." He said, "Ok, I'll nibble on it later." I said, "You didn't nibble on that chili I cooked for dinner." I know that the elderly lady in the back seat wanted to high five me, but I heard her chuckle a little. When we got home, Claxton fixed a bowl of chili and came into the basement where I was and said, "I want you to see me eating your chili otherwise, it was going to be a world war."

She was really trying hard to get his attention. At one of our banquets, she wore a sleeveless spaghetti strapped dress with no jacket or shawl. After the program was over, I saw her standing near Claxton, looking over her shoulders every few minutes to see if he was looking at her. The Lord brought it to my attention. What and who was she waiting for? He was busy shaking hands and thanking people for coming and she was steadily waiting.

When we finally left, we congregated in the lobby of the hotel, you know how we do, and we ended up standing outside in front of the hotel. Airika began walking to her car and then she yelled to Claxton as he was talking to the members, "Pastor! Quit watching me walk! I see you, you can't keep your eyes off of me." Everybody looked and she kept walking knowing that everybody was looking at her and thinking about what she had said. Claxton was too embarrassed. That statement was also made to make me think that she and Claxton had something going on.

Airika was surely called into the ministry. She heard "a" spirit calling her. After church on Sundays, Claxton stayed late to meet with people. Airika did not have transportation. She made Claxton believe that her heart went out for the senior citizens. She convinced him to let her use his car to go pray for the seniors.

Claxton did not consult with me. All I saw was a woman driving our other car and no one said anything to me about it. Airika knew her motives, but tricked Claxton. Though other women rode with her, it was the principle. She worked her way up to the President of the Ministerial Alliance.

Airika did a good job at becoming Claxton's friend. Why was my husband paying her rent when she was out of work? Why was my husband giving her money for gasoline? I heard Claxton say to her, "How are you doing on gas?" She said, "I'm alright Pastor. I'm alright?" He said, "Let me check because I know how you are." He literally got into her car to check. This was in the presence of two Deacons and the musician. I am still awaiting his entrance into my car to check my gasoline. I said to the musician, "How are you on your gasoline?" He said, "I'm on E." I said, "Me too." The Deacons laughed at me because they knew what I was doing. They knew that that wasn't right and they also knew that I was aware of the disrespect.

When I got home I told Claxton how disrespectful that was and incidents like that make silly, single, fickle women think that they are more worthy than your wife. He could not understand what I was talking about.

Pam stepped down from all of her positions at the church, Willimina and Claxton's friendship failed, this made Airika free willed now. She had a greater interest for the ministry. Claxton pumped her up. She was the MC at programs; she opened services in prayer, and worked the altar. I could not really focus on what she was saying because she was trying to be so intellectual and spiritual, but yet, rolling her neck and eyes and twisting her body as she spoke. She is the one that the news reporter would have as the spokesperson, reporting live at the scene of a crime that interrupted all television channels; and then have difficulty understanding her because of her tied tongue.

I have not been attending our church for quite some time now. I have pushed, prayed, and pressed with patience for over ten years. I deserve to worship at visiting churches in peace and with people who knows me not.

When fasting was no longer exercised and prayer services were no longer mandatory for the leaders, doors of unrighteousness poured in faster than a flood. Visiting speakers have told me personally that the sanctuary was thick with unclean spirits. I believe that when the people brought the unclean spirits into our church, they were never destroyed, though there was prayer. When sin is committed and no corrective action is taken or given, the sin multiplies. When sin is not dealt with, Saints become immune to it and it seems okay. If no one is saying anything about a matter, maybe it is okay. That seems true, but it's not.

When I was a teenager, I thought that shacking up was okay because everybody did it and no one was against it. If one person speaks, it can save the lives and the souls of many. The Lord asked in His Word, "Who will rise up for me against the evildoers? Or who will stand up for me against the workers of iniquity?" I answered and said, "I will, Lord?" This verse is found in Psalm 94:16.

Airika was diagnosed with cancer. When I heard the news, I was devastated. I immediately fasted for her healing. I called my friend, Karen Spencer, who has an awesome healing ministry and she also prayed. I'm just a servant for Jesus. She lost a lot of weight and her clothes were extremely too big. I then heard that Airika was healed and I rejoiced.

Sometimes the Lord afflicts us to warn us or to move us out of the way of hindering His work or both. Johoram did not live a holy and righteous life. Because of his ways, the Lord smote him in his bowels with an incurable disease and he died, II Chronicles 21:18-19, but read the entire chapter.

Because of my absence at the church, Airika boldly parks her rental car that my husband rents for her, in my parking spot at the church and sits on the pew that I normally sit on. She is telling people that she is going to be the next First Lady of Greater Power Pentecostal Church. Airika is a prime example of one who will sin without shame, concern, or consideration.

Do you know that Pastor Morgan picks her up in the mornings, drives himself to work, and she keeps our car all day long, then she picks him up in the evenings? During the week, she drives our Cadillac, on the weekends, he rents her a car, but he says that she pays for the rental because she doesn't have a credit card. She needs a Visa debit card to get her business straight.

I'm sure that you know by now that the doctor's have found cancer in other areas of her body? This is the time to fast and pray, not drive around in a Cadillac. I told Claxton, "You're so concerned about her losing her job by providing transportation; you need to be more concerned about her losing her soul." He thinks that he's doing a good deed for her and the Lord, but his wife has a problem with it. I don't have a problem with her driving our car; I have a problem with how things are done.

Airika is known for involving herself with married men; it's fascinating to her. If only more people would fear the wrath of God. If only more people would consider or foresee the reaping process or the harvest before they sow their seeds of discord. At the last appearance I made at Greater Power Pentecostal, I told Airika, as I was leaving, that I was going to call her. She said, "That'll never happen." You know her eyes were rolling, along with her neck, and she was loud, sitting on the front pew, during service. I had to leave because the spirits were too heavy for me and it was not the Holy Spirit.

Airika would look right silly if I called Cadillac roadside service to pick the car up from her job and have them take it some where, or report it missing or stolen. These are some of the things that I would have done years ago. The Lord said that vengeance is His. I trust His Word!

Chapter Ten

THE SPIRIT OF JEZEBEL

Willimina destroyed Claxton's ministry of marriage and family life outside of the church.

Pam destroyed Claxton's preaching ministry and reputation within the churches of our organization's District.

Airika destroyed Claxton's ministry within the church and his reputation within Greater Power Pentecostal Church.

They all desire power and control over people and they are all full of deception.

They all have Claxton believing that I dislike them. None of them spoke to me unless Claxton was in their view so that he could see them speaking to me.

They all have low self-esteem, with a touch of false humility and secret pride.

They all have tried to destroy me.

They have all played a part in standing between a God ordained married couple.

They have all stood between the works of God's ministry.

Surely they're not all to blame, but one thing for sure is that we ought to pray for strength for them to be able to handle their reaping, this includes Claxton.

Jezebel was the wife of King Ahab; she was evil, manipulative, controlling, a murderer, and a prophetess. This spirit is deeply rooted within our church. Every one wants to be the leader, but can't handle being a follower; they must be seen and heard. They believe that they can do as they're pleased because they are grown. They always have a word from their Lord to make Claxton think they are so prophetic and spiritually deep with revelation. Jezebels block the growth of ministries; anything that they touch does not prosper, it deteriorates. Auxiliaries with Jezebels as the President make themselves look busy, but are actually doing nothing. When they speak of their plans, it sounds like they have it together, but nothing materializes.

I encourage all Pastors to study the Jezebel spirit. There are too many books out for you not to know or recognize the spirit. My favorite book on Jezebel is entitled *Unmasking the Jezebel Spirit* by John Paul Jackson.

This book will teach you the characteristics of Jezebel and how to destroy the spirit. I have learned in this book that only the Pastor can unmask the Jezebel spirit. Tell other Pastors about the book or give it to Pastors as gifts. Please get it; it will bless you, your family, and your ministry.

Chapter Eleven

TWO PERSONALITIES

*A*fter a few years of pastoring, I noticed a drastic change in Claxton's voice, mannerisms, and behavior. As a child, my mother had favorite children and I was not one of them. She was so sweet to others, but not to me. I spent countless years trying to make my mom happy, it never happened.

In art class, all of my projects were made for her; that did not phase her, she was never satisfied. She helped everyone except for me. She did utilize my spiritual gifts to assist her in hiring employees for her company. Other than that, there was no relationship between us though I was crazy about her. I watched my mom's personalities switch from sweet waters to bitter waters before my very eyes. I loved to hear the sweet waters run as she cooked, baked, sang, prayed, prophesied, and laughed. But when those bitter waters began to flow, they were thick, dingy, and heavy.

I always believed that as long as I was suffering, she was okay with that. My mother was not interested in any of my most important events such as my graduation, my first wedding, and my baby shower. While I was waiting for my wedding to begin, she said, "I'll be glad when this mess is over." She has never celebrated my birthday with me. I did not have a cake as a child. She just didn't have money for me to get new clothes, shoes, senior pictures or anything.

Both my sister and I had our first child out of wed-lock while at home. I worked for the Government catching busses and taxis to work while my brother drove my baby to the sitter's. My mom hired a maid to help my sister raise her baby. My sister did not have a job and was not seeking employment. You didn't misunderstand what I just said and you don't have to re-read it. I said that we both had a baby, we both were unmarried, we both lived at home with Mama and Daddy. My mom hired a maid for my sister, and I worked and paid a babysitter. I often wondered if my mom's spirit had transferred to my husband's.

Claxton became extremely mean, selfish, and hateful. It was difficult living with someone who wore so many hats whereas I had difficulty distinguishing the hats. All of his words were sharp. I told him that his words are almost as sharp as the Word of God. I told him that the only difference is, his words don't cut and heal; they just cut and kill. Claxton's words kill the dinner; kill the shopping; kill the holiday; and kill the mood. I would plead the blood of Jesus during heated discussions in route to banquets. I asked the Lord to change the atmosphere in the car. All of a sudden, Claxton would stop yelling for a few minutes and then he'd start talking like he was degreed; talking as if there had been no yelling. When I say, "Heated discussion," that means that Claxton gets his clown on. I can't voice my thoughts because he loud talks me, tells me to shut up and then threatens me with, "If you say one more thing, I'll do something that you'll regret.

I listen to him change his voice from the "Pastor" sound which is slow, low, concerned, and compassionate to that other voice which is hard core, loud, ugly, mean, and cutting.

"Daughter, Jesus loves you. Everything is going to work out fine. Keep your head up. Don't give up. Trust the Lord with all of your heart, lean not unto thine own understanding. Stop by my office Sunday and tell me how things went. Okay, sweetheart. I'll see you then. Praise the Lord." I was just listening from the kitchen one day as Pastor Morgan consoled his bleeding sheep on the phone; that was so comforting to that woman. After all of those precious words to me from a man, I would make sure I'd meet him in his office. I probably would have said, "Why do we have to wait until Sunday? Can you meet me today?" As soon as Claxton hung up the phone, he turned into a "Click Clack." Click Clacks made nothing but meaningless noise. If the Click Clack clicked slowly, it was noisy. If the Click Clack clicked fast, it was noisy. Claxton clicked on me about anything and clacked on me right after preaching, right after counseling, right after a funeral, or right after praying.

When he rolls his eyes, it feels like a razor blade gliding across my chest. I learned that the rolling of the eyes is abuse. I don't understand why the members who are supposed to be so in tuned with Jesus; so powerful, so anointed, so prophetic, and so deep, why haven't they picked up on Claxton's two personalities?

Claxton has a bad temper. Everything frustrates him. When he walks into the house, he looks for things to complain about. He sometimes speaks with his teeth shut, but lips moving, gritting his teeth.

It has gotten to the point where I cannot stand listening to Pastor Morgan preach. He can really deliver the Word, he just doesn't live it. He is a different person at home.

Let me share a short story that will give you an example of my husband's personality change. One day I felt like some stove top, old-fashioned popcorn, popped in bacon grease and margarine. I asked Claxton if he wanted some and he said, "No." So I popped a small pot and took the bowl into the bedroom where we were.

I went back into the kitchen to wash the pot and top. When I returned to the bedroom, Claxton had eaten the entire bowl of popcorn. He said, "Girl, that popcorn was good." I went back into the kitchen, popped another pot, took it into the bedroom, went back to the kitchen to wash the pot and he ate that bowl of popcorn too. I popped some more and asked if he wanted more or not and he said, "No." I took the bowl into the bedroom, went back into the kitchen to wash the pot again.

When I went back into the bedroom, he was in bed under the cover. This was just about ten minutes later. I finally had a chance to sit down to enjoy the popcorn that I had the taste for.

As I was eating the first handful, Claxton turned over and said with the nastiest attitude, "I know that you are not crunching on that popcorn while I'm trying to go to sleep. That's rude! You know better than that! All you think about is yourself. Here I am trying to get some rest and you're crunching like you're crazy! I don't know what's wrong with you! I've got to get up in the morning and I can't sleep with all of that!" I was so mad. I couldn't believe it. I said, "It was okay for you to crunch, but now that I'm crunching, there's a problem? He said, "Yes! I don't see how you can't understand that." It rained popcorn in our bedroom because I threw the bowl. I was too out done.

As I was sitting in the chair in the living room, he got out of the bed to slam the door. Before he slammed it he said, "I knew that I was marrying a fool!" I was so mad that night. I was trying to get up out of the chair to respond to him marrying a fool, but the Lord would not let me get up. Every time I attempted to stand, the power of the Lord did not let me. I was stuck in the chair and eventually, I fell asleep.

To date, I have not told him what I was going to say that night. For some reason, the Lord didn't want me to respond. I don't know what would have happened. All I was going to say was, "At least you knew that you were marrying a fool; I was tricked. I didn't know that I was marrying a fool." That's all I wanted to say, but the Lord would not let me tell Claxton that.

Another example of two personalities:

Claxton would clown all week with me, the kids, the bills, responsibilities of any kind and then prepare sermons to preach for Sunday. Sometimes, I anxiously waited for him to preach. Do you know that he gathered incidents that occurred in the home that week and formed sermons? The interesting point that I'm trying to make is that he is the one who did the evil works all week long, but yet he preached against other folk engaging in such acts.

I thought that the Lord was whipping him by having him preach to himself about his own behavior. I thought that the message was convicting him and redirecting him. Sometimes, I would be smiling thinking that the change has come. Claxton had supporting scriptures, along with lyrics to hymns, and sometimes he'd stop in the middle of the message to praise the Lord. When we got back home, there were no changes; that was just an excellent message.

After several of those tricky messages, I said, "Just forget it, I'll understand one day." First, I thought that my husband was a hypocrite. Then it came to me that Pastor Morgan observed Claxton's behavior, whereabouts, and conversations all week, and then Pastor Morgan preached about Claxton to Claxton as he preaches to the church. Pastor Morgan knows the wrong doing of Claxton so he tries to minister to him on Sundays and Wednesdays because he knows that Claxton can't hear the Word any other time. Claxton does not have an interest in living holy, Pastor Morgan does.

I have over two million stories to share about Claxton. That was just two.

Chapter Twelve

MY MINISTRY

I was diagnosed with Motor Sensory Poly Neuropathy in the early 90's. Another name used is Charcot, Marie, Tooth Disease. It's a nerve disorder that caused me to lose feeling in my hands and feet. I can no longer reach into my purse and grab my comb because I can't feel it. I can't distinguish coins by feeling them, I have to see them. My hands and feet are consistently numb, stiff, and painful.

According to the United States Department of Defense, Social Security, and Neurology Specialists, I am disabled. I lose my balance when walking. I can't walk the halls of the malls like I used to.

There are countless things that I can no longer do. My ankles are weak whereas three sets of leg braces have been designed for me. My hands have lost strength immensely. I used to type over 100 words per minute, but now I type with two fingers. It is imperative that I get messages out to the people for the Lord.

Though I can't carry items in my hands as I used to, the Lord has blessed me to carry the Word every-where I go. I cannot stand for long periods of time as I used to, but the Lord has allowed me to stand firmly on His Word. I may not be able to fight with my hands as I once could, but the Lord gives me strength to fight in the Spirit.

I may not be able to sit for long periods of time as I once could, but I can be still and know that there is a God. I may not be able to exercise like I once did, but I can exercise my faith. I may not be able to clean my house as I used to, but I can keep my heart cleansed. I may not be able to walk for hours as I used to, but I can walk uprightly before the Lord. I may lose my balance, but the Lord will not allow me to stumble others. The Lord will enlarge my footsteps underneath my feet so that I slip not. I may not be able to run as I used to, but I've got to keep running with Jesus to see what the end will be; I can't stop now! My disability has given me the ability to feel more of the presence of the Lord. It has also caused me to be in a serene state of mind to hear the voice of the Lord even the more.

My ministry consists of winning souls to Jesus Christ through my writing. The Lord has blessed me to write Gospel songs. I hear instruments playing in my head, I see the choir singing and they only have mouths. I hear the sections of the choir singing their parts. The choir is always dressed in white. I tune in to read the lips of one choir member and that's how I get the lyrics to many of my songs.

I've learned about tithing through the lyrics of my songs. I've learned how to trust the Lord through the lyrics of my songs. I've learned not to be bitter towards people through the lyrics of my songs. I've learned that I could be cleansed with hyssop through the lyrics of my songs. The Lord is so awesome and so unique. He ministered to me through the lyrics of the songs that He gave me.

I have written 136 Gospel songs and 113 are already copyrighted. I have blood songs, choir songs, praise songs, worship songs, altar call songs, and a few anthems. The Lord told me that people were going to be calling me for songs. A thought was dropped in my spirit and that was to keep "writing" and "copyrighting."

When my mother was suffering with cancer, God gave me songs to comfort me when I stayed overnight at the hospital. He gave me songs while she was receiving chemotherapy. He gave me songs while she was receiving radiation treatments. When Claxton upset me, he'd leave the house and slam the front door. Before I could shed a tear, the Lord would give me a song. This is why we have to glory in our tribulations. There is good in suffering, though it hurts.

In my closet, I keep my perfume on the top shelf. As I'm reaching for my perfume and deciding on which fragrance to wear, the Lord gives me songs, every time I reach up. Would you call this the sweet smelling savor of Jesus?

I also write sermons. I have been writing sermons for years, but I thought that I was writing them for Claxton to preach. One early morning, I heard the Lord say to me, "Speak for Me." I knew that it was the Lord, but I looked over at Claxton and he was snoring. I said, "Lord, you know that I'm afraid to stand before Your people to speak." He said, "Fear Me more than you fear man." I said,

"Alright Lord." I thought that to speak for Him meant to testify more of His goodness, accept engagements requiring me to speak and to sing more. I asked some of my friends about what the Lord said and they told me that they knew, but they wanted the Lord to tell me. I didn't know what they were talking about and I was puzzled.

My prayer closet was the living room at that time. Every morning I took my Bible, a notebook, and a pen into my prayer closet. When I began to end my prayer, I had trouble. I could not end it, as I usually do, "And in all of these blessings I give You honor and glory in Jesus name, Amen." I could never get to that part. Somehow, I began teaching from a scripture I quoted, to the mirror, the chair, the couch, the front door, and the piano. It was like the Lord had taken over my prayer, my mouth, and my thoughts. When I realized what was happening, I stopped; I didn't understand. This went on everyday, for months. The devil is so tricky. He made me think that it was him (the devil), that did not want me to finish my daily prayer and because of that, I stopped praying for a while. I was so upset because I could not end my prayer properly. I tried to share this dilemma with Claxton, but I said to him, "I know a "woman" who….." I went on and detailed the story. I said, "Claxton, what does that mean?"

I thought that I was going to get a rhema word from the Pastor, first-hand. He said, "That ain't nothing, that woman ain't done nothing but stopped praying and started teaching, that's all. Tell her either she's going to pray or she's going to teach, she can't do them both at the same time." I also asked my fasting friends and they said, "I know, but I want God to tell you." But then I received revelation from the Lord. The Lord told me that the devil did not want me to teach His Word in the living room and that he was blocking me from both praying and teaching.

Today, after I pray, I still end up teaching. When I'm done teaching I say, "In Jesus Name, Amen." About a year later, I had a dream that I had gone grocery shopping late Saturday night. As I was leaving the store, I was held up at gun point. I said to the guy, "What do you want, my money, my purse, my keys, my car? What is it?" I said, "If you shoot me, I'll be with Jesus, can you say the same?" I went on ministering to him as the gun was to my head.

As I was speaking, people surrounded me to hear me. They were crying and yelling out, "I'll be at your church tomorrow, what's the name of it?" I said, "Greater Power Pentecostal!" Someone else yelled, "Where is it located?" I said, "737 S. Claxton Morgan Boulevard!" I was thinking to myself that they were not going to hear me; they were going to hear my husband. All while I was speaking, the guy still had the gun to my head and eventually, he broke down in tears and fell to the ground with his hands still on the trigger. That dream bothered me for so long because it had many meanings to it. One of my nieces gave me revelation of the dream. She said that I will be able to preach well under pressure. I asked my fasting friends about the dream and they said that they knew what it meant, but they wanted God to tell me. About a year later, I was driving with no music in the car. As I sat at the red light, the

Lord spoke to me and said, "Preach My Word." I dropped my head on the steering wheel. As I drove, I was waiting for fear to follow so that I could say, "I know that the Lord didn't say that because fear doesn't come from Him." The fear never came. Several different times throughout the day, I thought about what Jesus said to me earlier and awaited the fear, but it never came.

By the end of the day, I accepted the call into the ministry. I called my friends to share it with them and they all said the same thing which was, "I already knew that, I'm not surprised." My friends don't know each other and they live in different states. My one friend said, "You're the only one surprised." I was agitated by that. I was excited about telling my friends and they were like, "This is not news to us, you have been called a long time ago."

Of course Claxton doesn't believe that I've been called, but I can't concern myself with what man thinks when I know what God has said. To date, I have books and pamphlets that I've written for the church to equip the Saints with the knowledge of Jesus Christ; I'm in the process of publishing them. I have published teaching books that are blessings to all readers who desire to be closer to Jesus.

I have a prayer book for the youth that I'm working on and I have written packets for prayer seminars. In spite of all that I endure, Jesus equips me with His Word and I thank Him. The Lord told me that I have an abundance of writings because of my tithing. I have containers filled with notebooks of poems, songs, prayers, sermons, books, short stories, projects, ideas, scriptures, and revelation from the Lord. I had to purchase storage space to store the containers. Isn't that a promise from the Lord? Bring ye all the tithes into the storehouse, that there may be meat in mine house, and prove me now herewith, saith the LORD of hosts, if I will not open you the windows of heaven, and pour you out a blessing, that there shall not be room enough to receive it, Malachi 3:10. God's Word is true!

In a trance about eight years ago, the Lord said to me, "The job that I have given to Joseph is the same job I am giving unto you. Tell Claxton to tell you all about Joseph, he knows all about him." I called Claxton and told him what had happened and what the Lord had said. He told me that Joseph was a dreamer and a dream interpreter and no one believed his dreams. Claxton knew that I was also a dreamer and he himself did not believe my dreams. I had no knowledge of Joseph until then. I then studied Joseph's life and learned that his life was pretty much like mine. I was my dad's favorite girl. I am a dreamer and I have haters; folk have been trying to destroy me. Joseph had power, wisdom, and riches. Joseph was a dreamer, a supplier, a provider, and forgiving.

I have been in a pit for a long time. I just believe that the end of my fiery furnace must be near! When the heat diminishes, I'm going to step out of that furnace, as the Hebrew boys did in Daniel, Chapter 3 and all of the princes, governors, captains, and king's counselors will be gathered together to see that the fire that was upon me had no power. They are going to see that my hair was not singed (scorched), my coat was not changed (there was no need), and that I do not smell like smoke. Then they will say that there is no other God that can deliver like Jesus Christ can.

Chapter Thirteen

LONGSUFFERING

*L*ONGSUFFERING is a bitter piece of fruit that becomes sweet.

LONGSUFFERING is adversity, trials, tribulations, hard-times, troubles, problems, struggles, etc., that we encounter for a period of time that has no specific time limit on it. Whenever we suffer, whether one minute, one hour, or one day, it is long because it hurts. The length of time of our suffering is determined by God. However, the length of time suffered can be shortened if we follow God's route, but if we choose to follow our own route or agenda we surely will suffer indefinitely.

No one likes to suffer, but we must know that there are blessings in suffering.

Our troubles sometimes slip up on us (it's sometimes unexpected). At other times, our troubles are minor issues that we do not attack immediately which manifests into major issues due to procrastination. Some matters always seem irrelevant in the beginning, sort of like parking tickets. We forget to pay the ten dollar ticket, then it's doubled and tripled, then 300 dollars, court, warrant, boot on the tires; then arrest, and embarrassment. All of this torture for not mailing in ten dollars or for procrastinating.

Nevertheless, these troubles attach themselves to us

which makes the length of time seem extremely long because we're suffering.

Example – One minute of pain from a bleeding ankle
is long and it is long because we are suffering.

HOW TO HANDLE LONGSUFFERING

Thou therefore endure hardness, as a good soldier of
Jesus Christ, II Timothy 2:3.

A good soldier of Jesus Christ is one who is in the Army
of God, standing on the front line of the battlefield fully
dressed in his Army attire: The whole armor of God:

a. Loins girt about with truth – belt which holds all
of the armor up but also covers the loins. When
you are girded about with truth, it keeps a man
from morally sinning, it makes him behave Godly, he is sincere, and always on guard. His mind is
stayed upon Jesus and on things which are above.
The loins consist of the digestive system, the reproduction system, and the bowels. When they are
protected with truth, we are able to plant seeds of
truth in others and witness the reproduction of the
planted seeds.

b. Helmet of Salvation – the helmet is identification
of what army we belong. It protects our head from
the enemy which consists of the eyes, the mind, the
ears, and the mouth which are needed so that we

can hear, remember, and speak the laws, statutes, and commandments of God. The mind is the battlefield of the flesh and the spirit. The mind directs the usage of all of the armor. Our minds must be protected so that we won't entertain the thoughts of doubt, fear, and unbelief that the enemy brings. As the helmet defends the head, the hope of salvation defends the soul. Without the hope of victory, the soldier would not fight. Salvation will keep us during spiritual conflict and it will guard us from the blows which come from our enemy.

c. Breastplate of Righteousness consists of the heart, liver, and lungs. Wearing this armor gives us added protection to the loins enabling us to face the enemy with courage and without fear. Also, wearing this armor enables us to breathe the Word of God and exhale the Word of God (lungs). This armor protects our heart so that we will walk with motives that are pure, ponder words of God, and help us to do that which is right in God's eyesight.

d. The Shield of Faith is armor worn to protect the soldier's entire body. It was kept oiled to reflect the sun to blind the enemy and to deflect the enemy's blows. With this armor, we are protected from the fiery darts of doubt, fiery darts of fear, and the fiery darts of unbelief. We must remember that faith is believing what God has already said in His Word. Another analogy of faith is believing that the intangible is tangible. We must live by faith, not by sight and speak words of faith without doubting.

e. The Feet Shod with the Preparation of the Gospel
of Peace – our feet, because of the shoes, allows us
to stand in readiness; our feet represents our walk
with the Lord and the Gospel is the good news
that the Lord was crucified for our sins, buried,
and raised from the dead by God and yet lives today, and inside of us. Peace is freedom from strife.
With these shoes, we are prepared to walk in peace,
walk in holiness, walk uprightly before God and we
will not be moved from the Gospel and neither will
we be ashamed of the Gospel of Jesus Christ. With
our feet set securely in the peace of the Lord's, we
are ready to move in the direction that the Holy
Spirit leads us. We can also tread boldly on our enemies turf standing head to head and toe to toe to
the enemy proclaiming the power in Jesus and setting captives free.

f. The Sword – The Word of God – The Sword of the
Spirit can only be applied effectively when all of the
other pieces of armor are on. The Word of God is
the foundation of the world. For in the beginning
was the Word and the Word was with God, and
the Word was God. The Word became flesh. The
Word is true; the Word of the Lord is pure; the
Word is powerful; the Word cuts and heals at the
same time; the Word is a weapon that God gave us
authority to use because it is sharp; sharper than
any two-edged sword. So speak the Word, Pray the

Word, teach the Word, sing the Word, read the Word, study the Word, meditate on the Word, and believe the Word, Ephesians 6:11-17.

While we're on the front line of the battlefield, fully dressed in our armor, we must:

a. Praise the Lord – For all He's done

b. Worship the Lord – for who He is

c. Pray – without ceasing – pray the scriptures

d. Fast – abstain from food/pleasures for God (on your own)

e. Meditate – day and night

f. Consecrate – set yourselves apart from friends, family, telephone

During our suffering, we are sometimes encouraged with these comforting words:

There is light at the end of the tunnel!

Well, the Lord gave me revelation of this familiar statement of ease. He said that there is light inside of the tunnel because He is light and He cannot be hidden in darkness. Darkness and light are both alike unto Him……. Yea, the darkness hideth not from thee; but the night shineth as the day: the darkness and the light are both alike to thee, Psalm 139:12. In our darkest hour, we must remember that Jesus is with us. Didn't He promise that He'd never leave us or forsake us? The psalmist says.....The LORD is on my side; I will not fear: what can man do unto me? Psalm 118:6. If the Lord is on the Palmist's side, then surely is He on our side. Encourage someone today with, "The Lord is on your side."

Two scriptures that really comfort me are:

And not only so, but we glory in tribulations also: knowing that tribulation worketh patience; And patience, experience; and experience, hope: And hope maketh not ashamed; because the love of God is shed abroad in our hearts by the Holy Ghost which is given unto us, Romans 5:3-5.

These things I have spoken unto you, that in me ye might have peace. In the world ye shall have tribulation: but be of good cheer; I have overcome the world, I John 16:33.

Chapter Fourteen

ASPIRING FIRST LADIES

*M*inisters' wives who desire to be a First Lady or single women desiring to marry a Pastor must know that this is a fiery furnace that you want God to place you in. This furnace is hot and this is because you have to increase your prayer life and consecrate yourself more. You have to let go of some friends and family members to work for Jesus. You have to correct, recommend, warn, direct, rebuke, instruct, and counsel people who are unwilling to listen to you.

You have to love those who hate you. You have to encourage people who degrade you. You have to pray for those who despitefully use you. You have to smile inspite of, hug when you know the person can't stand you, visit the sick and shut in when you know that they only want to see the Pastor and not you, donate money to be placed in greeting cards of those who have stepped on you. You must exemplify Jesus Christ in all areas of your life, inside and outside of the church whether it's in conversations (the words that you implant in others); music (lyrics that you allow to rest in your spirit); disagreements (words you choose to say); behavior (leaving the aroma of Jesus wherever you go); appearance (modestly dressed); relationships (honest, kind, compassionate, giving, and lovable); deeds (doing all that you do for the Lord); purchases (being a good steward over money God entrusts you with); and advice (giving Godly counsel).

If you possess unclean spirits such as envy, jealousy, control, deception, covetousness, pride, or anger, then your tenure as a First Lady will be short. It will be short because you will run many members away from the church. If there are no members, how can your husband Pastor? Who will be there for him to Pastor? I encourage you to develop a stronger relationship with the Lord because you won't be able to stand the fiery darts of the enemy without your weapons which are fasting, prayer, praise, worship, consecration, and meditation, along with putting on your whole armor of God, Ephesians 6:11.

Chapter Fifteen

THE POTENTIAL FIRST LADIES

*P*lease learn today that First Ladyship is a position that God equips you for and there are no training sessions nor lessons; we learn by trial and error or by trials and tribulations. Lay members try to tell you how to be a First Lady, but they don't know. First Ladies can give you tips, suggestions, and ideas, but they may not be helpful to you for your ministry.

I know that I have had many interesting stories that you've read, but that doesn't mean that you will have the same experiences. You may not experience half of my dilemmas. Don't get me wrong though, you will be tested and tried. On the other hand, there are some good benefits. What I really like about First Ladyship is that because husbands and wives are one, Jesus equips the wife with revelation, compassion, understanding, and wisdom as He does the husband. She has to encourage her husband and minister to him. These blessings I believe are given to the soul winning First Ladies. All First Ladies are not soul winners. For the Word to read, "He that winneth souls is wise," means that every one is not wise and every one is not winning souls, but he that does is wise.

Another great benefit is that the First Lady is in the position to lead women in holiness and to lead women to holiness. She is the example that Jesus prepared to stand by her husband and to assist him in ministry. There are other benefits like anniversary services, vacations, conventions, greeting card showers, holiday gifts, and special seating. Though First Ladyship looks glamorous because of her fine hats, clothing, jewelry, special seating, vehicles, and homes, she has to live holy just like everyone else. There may be special seating at banquets, anniversary services, conventions, councils, and dinners at the church for her, but there is no special seating for the "First Lady" or the "Lady" or the "Pastor's Wife," or the "Co-Pastor" in Heaven. She has to enter Heaven just like the delivered drug addict, the delivered prostitute, the delivered alcoholic, the delivered pimp, the delivered thief, the delivered murderer, and the delivered rapist.

First Ladies may be exempt from paying dues to the auxiliary she is involved in and she may be exempt from purchasing tickets for the church's fund raising dinner, but we are not exempt from temptation and neither are we exempt from repenting, apologizing, admitting wrong doing, controlling the Saints, mistreating others, or engaging in sin. We are not to be leaders only; we must be followers of the Word too.

If your husband is holding an Assistant Pastor's position and it looks as if your husband is going to be the next shepherd or he's in training to be the next shepherd, this is the time for you to fast even the more and pray for wisdom. If your husband has already been unctioned by the Lord to be a shepherd, I encourage you to do the same.

Ladies, there is a tear forming under that beautiful hat

you're anxiously waiting to wear on Sunday. There is a tear to be rolled as you sit in your special seat. There is a tear to drop on your custom made outfit. There is a tear glistening down your face when the holiest Saints of God deceive you. There will be showers of tears throughout the entire ministry. Some tears will be tears of joy; some, tears of sorrow; some, tears of pain; some, tears of praise; some, tears of worship; and some, tears of complexity. Know this day that - The Pastor's Wife Does Cry!

A NOTE TO THE PASTORS

*P*astors, I don't have any pastoral advice for you from a personal angle; I wish I did. I will say this, when Pastors are older, we don't see as much foolishness within his church. This is why we hear parishioners saying, "We don't have all of that trouble in our church like other churches have, our Pastor will get you together." That's good to hear and it's good to know. Oh, but when Pastor was younger, we don't know what he endured. But know that Pastor learned. Pastor gained knowledge. Pastor acquired wisdom. Pastor developed patience from tribulations. Pastor obtained experience. Pastor attained understanding. Pastor grew.

Younger Pastors, find out why your wife is crying and assist her. You don't have to ask her if she cries or not, just ask her what's wrong or what's bothering her. We don't always want to share with our husbands our troubles because we think that they will think that our troubles are petty. Pastors, though your wife may be busy with the kids, their homework, their troubles, their doctor visits, practice and games, the home, cooking, cleaning, and shopping, the bills, the church or whatever; the bottom line is that she cries. Yes, we are strong and yes, we can handle a multitude of responsibilities simultaneously, but we still shed tears.

Pastors, when folk approach you with issues concerning your wife, let them know that the two of you are one.

If the matter is true or not right, please address your wife in private. Let the devil know that his scheme, scam or scandal isn't working on this day that the Lord has made. Let that devil know that you will rejoice and be glad.

It doesn't matter if the members turn their backs on your wife, though we would love for peace and harmony to rule always within the church, but we know the truth. But when her husband takes sides with others, even if it's the in-laws, it's not good business practice. Let no one divide you; Satan doesn't like unity!

Remember Pastors......The Pastor's Wife Does Cry!

Chapter Seventeen

DEPRESSION

My husband was diagnosed with depression before I met him. I did not know the seriousness or the severity of depression. After intense study, I've learned something very interesting. Pastor Claxton William Morgan has justification for all of his unrighteousness. Based upon the symptoms of the many forms of depression or mental illness, Claxton's behavior is found.

A Few Forms of Depression or
Mental Illness are:

Schizophrenia   Dysthymia
Dysphoria   Bi Polar Type I
Bi Polar Type II   Cyclothymia
Psychopath   Sociopathy
Antisocial Personality   Alienated Sociopathy
Disorder   Delusional Disorder

Some Symptoms for these Disorders are abnormal social behavior, deceitfulness, manipulativeness, impulsiveness, poor planning, irritability, aggressiveness, irresponsibility, no remorse after hurting, mistreating, or stealing from others, charming, false sense of self-worth, pathological lying, cunning, lack of sympathy, freeloading, refusal to accept responsibility for own actions, racing thoughts, can't concentrate well, need little sleep, unrealistic beliefs in one's abilities and powers, poor judgment, spending sprees, abuse of alcohol and sleeping medications, and denial that anything is wrong.

Some suffer from paranoia and it is characterized by delusions (false beliefs held by a person despite evidence to the contrary).

Depression causes aches and pains; headaches, stomachaches, and joint pain. Some have gastrointestinal trouble like indigestion and constipation.

All of this information can be found on the internet under the following websites:

1. allaboutdepression.com

2. healthline.com

3. healthology.com

4. psychologytoday.com

5. faculty.ncwc.edu/toconnor/428/428lect16. htm

There are many forms of depression. Take the time to study the illness. You'll find help for your loved one. You may find help for yourself! Depression is an attack of the mind. An attack of the mind is demonic. It's the mind that Satan wants; it's his only entrance into us. But, Jesus is still a Healer today! I believe that medication may be needed so that one can think rationally.

When a person is in denial about his illness or believes that he is normal, then he has nothing to pray about in that area because in his mind, he's alright. If we confess our sins, he is faithful and just to forgive us our sins, and to cleanse us from all unrighteousness, I John 1:9. If a person believes that he is okay, why would he confess? This is why I believe that after medication is taken, his thoughts are not racing and he's able to think clearly. I believe that this is when permanent healing by Jesus takes place.

I smoked two packs of cigarettes per day. I tried to stop smoking because others had a problem with it; I didn't. When I decided to seriously stop, I wrote down the pros and cons of smoking. I had more cons than pros. I took the pros and narrowed down what I loved most about my cigarettes; it was the aroma. I then thought of the worst discomfort for me to endure and that was nausea. The Lord told me to take to prayer "the aroma" and "the nausea." My prayer was for the Lord to nauseate me whenever I smelled cigarettes.

After prayer, I went to the store to buy some nicotine gum. I had no desire for a cigarette. While I was chewing the third or fourth piece of gum, the Lord spoke to me and said, "I'm Greater than the gum." I have not had a cigarette since. Feel free to use my prayer technique to help you to overcome some of your strongholds. My point here is, because I was so busy smoking and going on doing my usual, I wouldn't have been able to hear the Lord speaking to me. The gum relaxed me and calmed me down for a minute to hear the Lord's few, but powerful Words.

I have said all of that to say that I believe that it's okay to take medication until a person's thinking process is calm. I believe that they will be in a better position to make decisions, notice strange behavior, conscious of hurting others, likable, and more considerate. I believe when a person is free from racing thoughts, negative thoughts or feelings of people; and with a sound mind, then the Healing from Jesus will come.

I am not saying that Jesus can't or won't heal us without medication because He can do all things! Also, prayer is always in order; in order in our spirits. In other words, we are to always have the spirit to pray. No, we can't go to the museum, take the microphone and begin to plead the blood of Jesus because prayer is in order, but we can pray to ourselves. There can never be too much prayer in our own private prayer lives.

Chapter Eighteen

REJECTION AND ABUSE

I don't think that a person ever gets comfortable with rejection. I always believed that situations cannot stay the same. Rejection is good for us but mental and emotional abuse needs to be addressed.

There's always a lesson to be learned with everything that's done to us, even if the lesson is for us to recognize abuse in others or to teach us not to behave accordingly. If you notice that your loved one or your spouse doesn't want you to advance, acquire, laugh, share, assist, go places, or do things, look into that. If your loved one blocks you, especially in ministry, he has to face and answer to Jesus; don't worry about it.

My husband has no interest in my books. He says that they will go no where and that they are nothing but filth. He says, "All you do is write crazy songs that no one wants to hear." He says, "All you do is fast all of the time and it just doesn't make sense." He says, "All you do is speak in those old crazy tongues." He says, "The worst thing that I hate is when I come up to the pulpit, take my seat, and look over and see your ugly face." He says, "You're a disgrace to all women." He says, "All you do is have all of those crazy dreams which don't come from God. You need to quit eating all of those late night snacks." He says, "Why do you think that God is always talking to you? God will speak to me first before He speaks to you, I'm the head!"

Aren't these precious words that my husband speaks to me? These are encouraging lines that he uses when he's upset. These are also statements that he shares with some of my personal friends about me.

I was the President of the After Care Ministry that I formed. I fasted and prayed for wisdom to master the program. We took care of the new member's needs (personal and spiritual), we prayed with them, developed relationships with them, and accurately documented every action taken. I composed the duties and responsibilities for seven coordinators. I trained them and provided them with documents to be completed and submitted to me weekly. I composed the forms with carbons so that the Pastor was aware of the status of his new members.

After all of that hard-work, Pastor Morgan removed me from the ministry. He demanded me to train one of the ministers. He invited the minister over to our home and told me to turn over all of the forms, job descriptions, and new members telephone numbers. He said that I wasn't doing anything with the ministry. The minister said that it was too much work for him so he gave it back to me. Pastor Morgan refused to let me handle the ministry so he then gave it to one of the other ministers. This Ministry is now in *suppression.*

I was forming a Women's Ministry that was going to bring us together as a true church family. I fasted and prayed for direction. I wrote books for the ministry. We were going to do a lot of "fasting" and "casting." I was told by Claxton that as long as I wouldn't take Sunday school students out of their classes, Sunday mornings would be a good day for us to meet. I had gathered 18 students who had stopped coming to church, gained Holy boldness to teach each week, and I made the announcement. Low and behold, Pastor Morgan cancelled the ministry. He said that we didn't need that kind of ministry. So many people were looking forward to the ministry forming.

About six months later, Claxton's niece asked if she could form the ministry. He immediately said, "Yes! That's the best idea that anyone could have came up with." His niece said that Claxton said, "You brought tears to my eyes." When he learned from her that she was just asking if it was okay for the ministry to be formed, but I was really going to be over it, he was upset. Claxton said to me, "I didn't know that you had something to do with it." Well, this Ministry went into *repression.*

I was going to be over the outreach ministry a few years back. That ministry consisted of picking up the homeless from the shelters, providing them with snacks, breakfast, lunch, clothes, training classes, rehabilitation, Bible class, and more. I fasted and prayed for direction in the ministry.

There was also another lady who was going to work with me. I was waiting for our first meeting to begin because I had so much information to share. I found out that Pastor Morgan had already had the first meeting, the second meeting, and the third meeting as well. He had taken over the entire outreach ministry and did not tell me that I was pushed over and pushed out of the way. He took over! After a bout a year, you know that the Outreach Ministry went into *recession*.

I formed the New Member's classes. I prayed and fasted for direction with this ministry. I wrote six books which took four years of study, research, and meditation to complete. The course was designed to last six weeks long. Each week, there was a different instructor to teach for one hour from one of my books. The students were grateful for all that they had learned. The books were written with information that I needed and wished I had when I was a new saint.

The first class had 32 students and they faithfully came out each week. One evening, during class time, I had run upstairs to the office to get some supplies and Pastor Morgan was sitting in the front of the sanctuary looking disturbed. I walked over to him and said, "What's wrong?" He said, "This is the first time, in the history of me being at this church, that the church has been packed with people and there is no service. When I pulled up on the lot, the lot was full. I have not seen anything like this and I've been here over 30 years." Men and women helped me in the kitchen with the serving of refreshments, setting-up of the tables, and with cleaning up. Claxton couldn't believe the support that I had.

We had a beautiful graduation at the end of the year for all of the new members who had completed the course.

The graduation was anointed and the church was packed. When the next New Member's classes began, Pastor Morgan cancelled the refreshments. I kept trying to explain to him that the students rushed to the class from work without going home first and that they were hungry. That didn't matter to him. He said that they couldn't eat and learn at the same time. Even though the refreshments were cancelled, the helpers still came out and so did the students. Well, Pastor Morgan removed me from the New Member's Ministry and of course this ministry is in ***depression.***

There are countless ideas and suggestions that I have given that are still in operation, but no one knows, but Pastor Morgan. I visited the sick and shut-in with him. I attended funerals and weddings with him. He replaced me with others.

I have said all of that to say that Pastor Morgan has members believing that I have no interest in helping him in the ministry. They don't know the truth. They don't know that Claxton has cancelled or shut down any work that the Lord has given me. They think that because I'm absent, that I am purposely trying to destroy his ministry, I don't have that kind of heart. I want the best for him.

The Saints believe what their Pastor tells them which is good in a sense. In the Bible, though the people were taught by great men of God, they still searched the scriptures for themselves. In Pastor Morgan's messages, he says that he's tired of fighting and that he's going to have to make some changes. That is nothing but deception. He has the people thinking that I am at home fighting and clowning with him and they believe him. He's believed by the members because I'm quiet at the church and they are probably thinking that I'm a mess at home. That's not right to fool the Saints or the aint's like that. I'll tell anyone, "If you want to know the truth of any matter, ask the children."

Abuse is not just physical! Most physical wounds will heal, but emotional, verbal, and mental wounds are deeply cut and these scars must be healed by Jesus. I have been cut by man and blessed to be healed by Jesus. I'll always believe that Jesus is and will always be my Strength, my Protector, my Guide, my Hope, my Refuge, my Comfort, and my Healer.

CONCLUSION

To all Pastors, Executive Boards, Board of Directors, Deacons, Auxiliary Presidents, Vice Presidents, Ministers, Finance Leaders, Musicians, Office Workers, Nurses, Ushers, Mother's Board, Audio Visual Leaders, Prayer Warriors, Janitors, Security Guards, Choir Members, Praise Dancers, New Members, Transportation Drivers, Lay Members, Absent Members, and Visitors, Always Remember that..........

THE PASTOR'S WIFE DOES CRY!

To the women who are envious or jealous of your Pastor's wife, always rolling your eyes at her, excluding her, degrading her, and openly disrespectful, I pray that you apologize to her and ask God for forgiveness. Try to learn all that you can from her because she's priceless and you're missing out. She may be the prayer warrior for your troubles. She may have that rhema word for you. She may have the answers to your most difficult questions, you won't know until you change. To you who love your Pastor's wife, I personally thank you. God has a blessing for you!

SCRIPTURES TO COMFORT YOU!

Upon the wicked he shall rain snares, fire and brimstone, and an horrible tempest: this shall be the portion of their cup, Psalm 11:6.

The eyes of the LORD are upon the righteous, and **his ears are open** unto their **cry**, Psalm 34:15.

The righteous **cry**, and the **LORD heareth, and delivereth them** out of all their troubles, Psalm 34:17.

Hear my prayer, O LORD, and give ear unto my **cry**; hold not thy peace at my tears, Psalm 39:12.

I waited patiently for the LORD; and **he inclined unto me,** and heard my **cry**, Psalm 40:1.

Evening, and morning, and at noon, will I pray, and cry aloud: and **he shall hear my voice**, Psalm 55:17.

When I **cry** unto thee, then shall mine enemies turn back: this I know; for God is for me, Psalm 56:9.

Let my prayer come before thee: incline thine ear unto my **cry**, Psalm 88:2.

Nevertheless he **regarded their affliction**, when he heard their **cry**, Psalm 106:44.

Let my **cry** come near before thee, O LORD: give me understanding according to thy word, Psalm 119:169.

They that sow in tears **shall reap in joy**, Psalm 126:5.

Though I walk in the midst of trouble, **thou wilt revive me**: thou shalt stretch forth thine hand against the wrath of mine enemies, and thy right hand shall save me, Psalm 138:7.

The LORD will perfect that which concerneth me: thy mercy, O LORD, endureth for ever: forsake not the works of thine own hands, Psalm 138:8.

He will **fulfill the desire** of them that fear him: he also will hear their **cry**, and will save them, Psalm 145:19.

Blessed be God, even the Father of our Lord Jesus Christ, the Father of mercies, and the God of all comfort; Who **comforteth us in all our tribulation**, that we may be able to comfort them which are in any trouble, by the comfort wherewith we ourselves are comforted of God, II Corinthians 1:3-4.

And he said unto me, My grace is sufficient for thee: for **my strength is made perfect in weakness**. Most gladly therefore will I rather glory in my **infirmities**, that the power of Christ may rest upon me. Therefore I take pleasure in **infirmities**, in reproaches, in necessities, in **persecutions**, in **distresses** for Christ's sake: for when I am weak, then am I strong, II Corinthians 12:9-10.

My brethren, **count it all joy** when ye fall into divers temptations. Knowing this, that **the trying of your faith worketh patience**. But let patience have her perfect work, that ye may be perfect and entire, wanting noth-

Blessed is the man that **endureth** temptation: for when he is tried, he **shall receive the crown of life**, which the Lord hath promised to them that love him, James 1:12.

And who is he that will harm you, if ye be followers of that which is good? But and **if ye suffer for righteousness' sake, happy are ye:** and be not afraid of their terror, neither be troubled, I Peter 3:13.

And **God shall wipe away all tears** from their eyes; and there shall be no more death, neither sorrow, nor crying, neither shall there be any more pain: for the former things are passed away, Revelation 21:4.

ing, James 1:2-4.

REFERENCES:

King James Version of the Bible

Unmasking the Jezebel Spirit – John Paul Jackson

Various Websites:

www.allaboutdepression.com

www.healthline.com

www.healthology.com

www.psychologytoday.com

www.faculty.ncwc.edu/toconnor/428/428lect16.htm

Printed in the United States
217268BV00001B/4/A